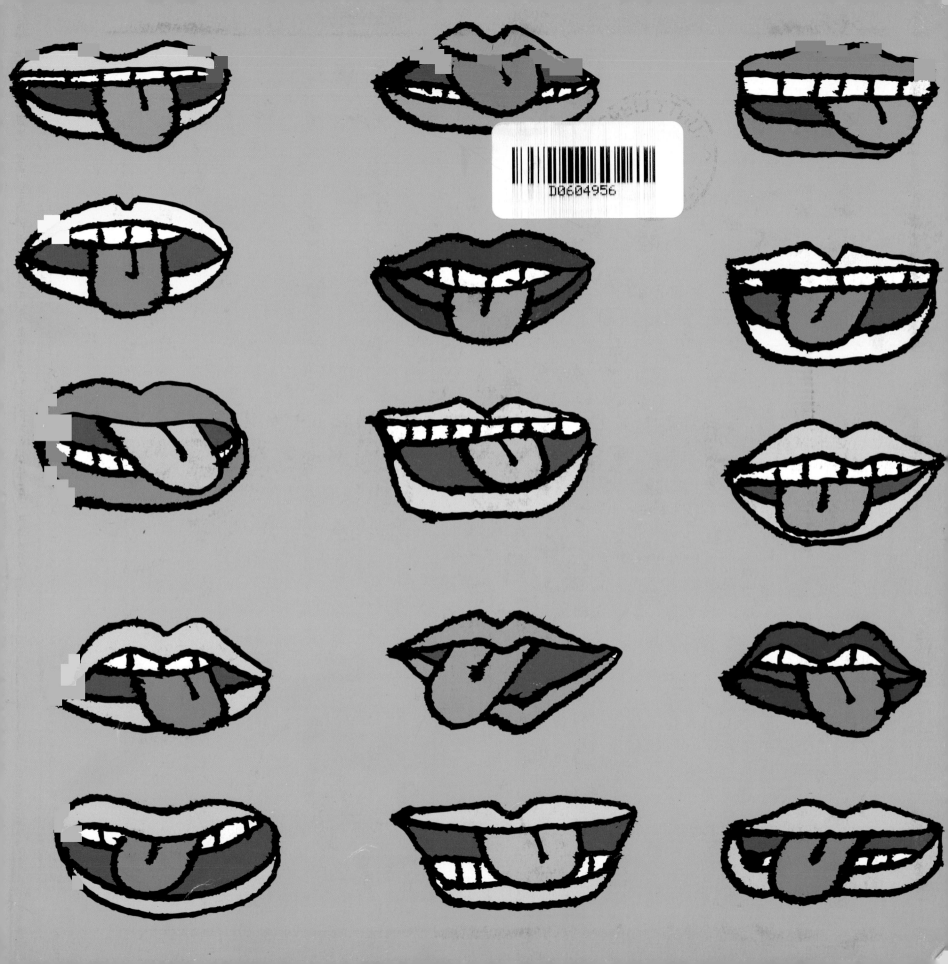

THE TONGUE TWISTER

is a phrase or sentence that is difficult to articulate because of a sequence of similar sounds. They should be spoken and repeated several times, quickly without mistake. As a form of speech therapy, it helps in the treatment of some speech defects.

She Sells Seashells

ILLUSTRATED BY
Seymour Chwast

APPLESAUCE PRESS

Kennebunkport, Maine

She sells seashells by the seashore.

Sally Swan
swims to Will.
Wally Swan
swims away.

If Shep chews shoes,
what shoes should
he choose to chew?

Cheery
chickens cooking
in the kitchen.

Cleopatra's mattress has patches.

Hobnob with the nasty neighbor? Never!

Bears are bored by bloated boars.

The gargling gargoyle gargles with glee.

Giddy gladiators grow gladiolas.

Watching the clocks and winding wristwatches.

Mark mocks
the merry
mockingbird.

My Swiss
miss misses
Mississippi.

Awful old Ollie oils oily autos.

Phillip
flips fine
flapjacks.

Bobby's bobbling baby buggy.

Selma went swimming in her swell swimsuit.

Fred,
the friar, frying
flounder.

Stanley
sips Samantha's
soup.

Cheryl's sister slipped on skis and skinned her knees.

The merry moose of Manitoba wears moccasins from Minnetonka.

Lazy cows
gather to graze on
green grass.

Chuck eats cheap Chinese.

The zitherist plays his sister's zither.

Washington washes his britches with dishes.

Carla's charming car is chocolate.

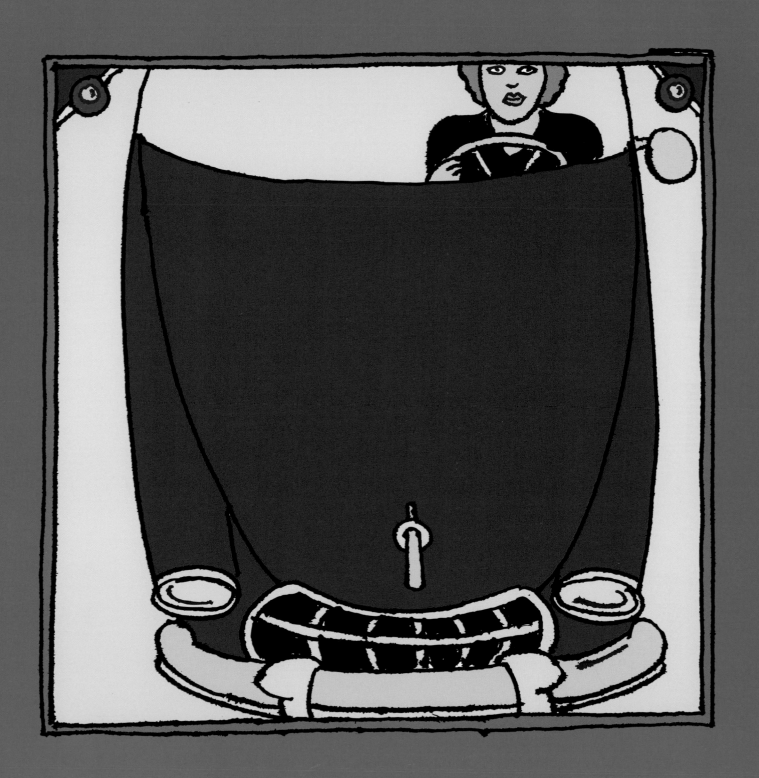

ABOUT APPLESAUCE PRESS

Good ideas ripen with time. From seed to harvest, Applesauce Press strives to bring fine reading, information, and entertainment together between the covers of its creatively crafted books. Our Cider Mill bears fruit twice a year, publishing a new crop of titles each Spring and Fall. Applesauce Press is an imprint of Cider Mill Press Book Publishers.

Visit us on the web at
www.cidermillpress.com

or write to us at 12 Port Farm Road
Kennebunkport, Maine 04046

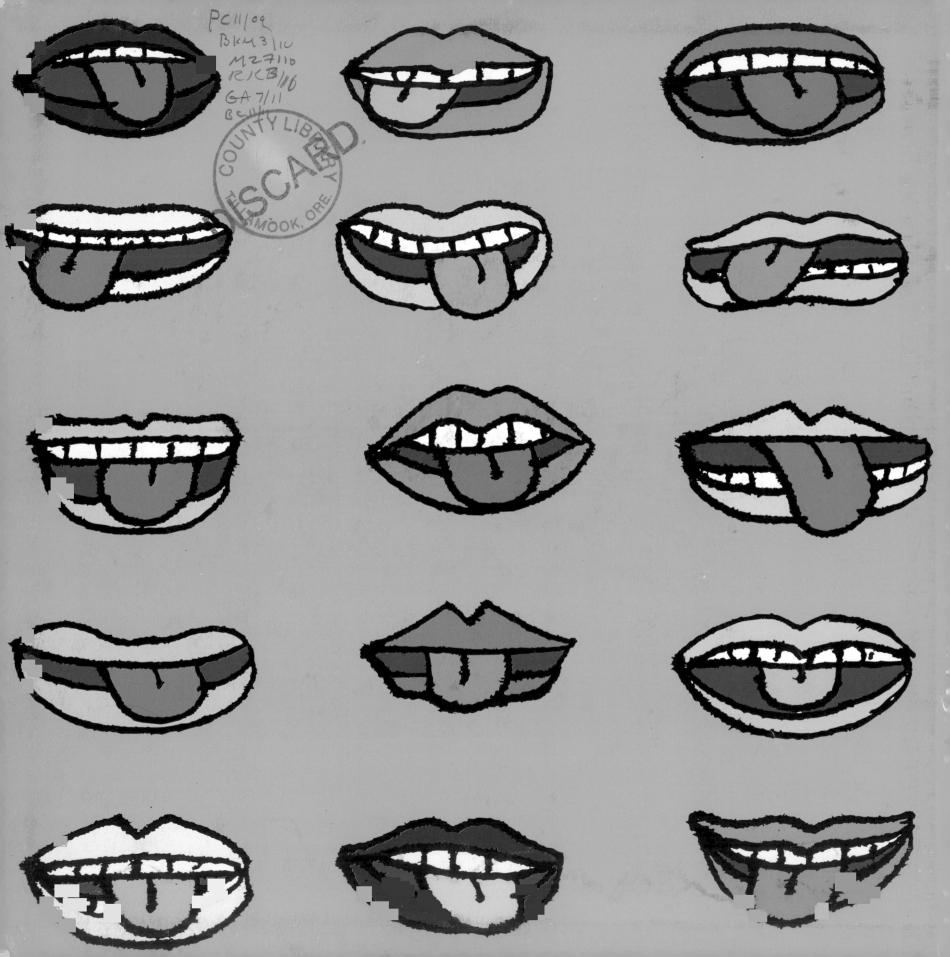